MUSIC

www.thewhybooks.co.uk

Illustrations by Charity Russell
www.charityrussell.com

Where Are All The Black Female Composers?

The Ultimate Fun Facts Guide

NATHAN HOLDER

Illustrated by Charity Russell

HOLDERS HILL

CONTENTS

INTRODUCTION

In most of the books you read about classical composers, you will learn about Bach, Beethoven, Chopin or Mozart.
But not in this book!

There are so many more composers who don't look like the men we've all heard about! And many of them are Black women who have written music that has brought joy to people all over the world.

Join Zaki, Olivia, Callum and Phoebe as they take a look at Black women who have composed some of the most amazing music you'll ever hear!

WHAT IS A COMPOSER?

A composer is someone who organises sounds!
In the past, composers have used ink, pencils and paper, but now, many use special computer programs to create and arrange the sounds they want. Although Black women have written a lot of music in many different genres such as pop, jazz and rock, this book focuses on some Black women who have written in a classical or neo-classical style. These styles include operas, concertos, symphonies, theatre and film scores.

CHIQUINHA GONZAGA
(1847–1935)
Rio de Janeiro, Brazil

Gonzaga was not only a Brazilian composer but also the first recognised female conductor in her country. Her main instrument was the piano, and she composed her first piece at age 11. After a turbulent marriage, she devoted her time to composition, and over the course of her life, she composed more than 2,000 pieces, including tangos, waltzes, operas and mazurkas. In 1917, she created the first society for copyright protection in Brazil called The Brazilian Society of Theatrical Authors (SBAT).

Gonzaga continued composing up until the final years of her life, and her operetta *Forrobodó* (1911) is still regarded as one of the best Brazilian shows of the genre.

On 17 October 2018, Google honoured her and her many achievements with her own Google Doodle.

CATALINA BERROA (1849-1911)
AMANDA ALDRIDGE (1866-1956)
ANNA GOODWIN (1874-1959)

'Atraente' (1877)

'Gaúcho' (1895)

'Ó Abre Alas' (1899)

NORA HOLT
(c.1885–1974)
Kansas City, Kansas, U.S.A.

It's unclear exactly when she was born, but Holt started learning how to play the piano at 4, and she was soon playing the organ in her local church. With her father, she co-wrote the school song for Western University and graduated from that same University in 1917. She went on to become the first African American to earn a master's degree in music composition.

Holt has more than 200 works to her name. She was an important member of the Harlem Renaissance—an exceptionally creative era in the 1920s in Harlem, New York, which saw many musicians, writers, performers and artists expressing themselves through the arts.

She hosted her own radio show called *Nora Holt's Concert Showcase*, and later in life, she became the first African American elected to the Music Critics Circle of New York. Unfortunately, only two of her compositions have survived. The others were stolen from her storage unit.

'Negro Dance' (1921)

'The Sandman'

Rhapsody on Negro Themes

FLORENCE PRICE
(1887–1953)
Little Rock, Arkansas, U.S.A.

Price was a musical prodigy. She gave her first performance when she was only 4 years old and wrote her first composition at 11. She was a well-respected teacher and was appointed head of music at Clark Atlanta University. Amongst her many achievements, Price had her *Symphony in E minor* performed by the Chicago Symphony in 1933, which made her the first African American woman to have a composition performed by a major orchestra. She also worked closely with another African American composer, Margaret Bonds, and the poet Langston Hughes.

The Florence B. Price Elementary School was named after her in 1964, and, since her death, her works such as *Concerto in One Movement* have been performed and recorded more and more. The first International Florence Price Festival was announced in 2019, but due to COVID-19, the festival will be held in 2021.

Symphony No.1 (1931–32) ♪

Three Little Negro Dances (1933)

Violin Concerto No. 2 (1952)

HELEN EUGENIA HAGAN

(1891–1964)

Hagan is recognised as the first African American woman to earn a degree from the Yale School of Music. She composed and taught piano for many years. Unfortunately, only one of her compositions have survived.

L. VIOLA KINNEY (c.1890–1945)

My Spirituals (1927)

The Life of Christ in Negro Spirituals (1931)

Paradise Lost and Regained (1934)

EVA JESSYE
(1895–1992)
Coffeyville, Kansas, U.S.A.

Jessye grew up in church, first listening to church choirs, then directing a quartet that she set up before she was 13. Like Nora Holt, she studied at the Western University in Kansas, then moved to New York in 1922 to work for a newspaper and conduct vocal groups.

Jessye worked as a choir director for the film *Hallelujah!* in 1929, and for the opera *Four Saints in Three Acts* in 1933. In 1935, based on her expertise in arranging Negro spirituals and choir direction, she was hired by George Gershwin to conduct choirs for his renowned opera *Porgy and Bess*.

She was active in the American civil rights movement, and marched with Dr. Martin Luther King Jr. One of the groups she led became the official choir for The Great March On Washington in 1963, where Dr. King delivered his historic "I Have a Dream" speech, calling for an end to racism. Not long before she died, she set up the Eva Jessye African-American Music Collection at the University of Michigan where she had taught for many years.

SHIRLEY GRAHAM DU BOIS
(1896–1977)
Indianapolis, Indiana, U.S.A.

Du Bois grew up in a politically active and religious family. In 1928, she travelled to France to study music composition and orchestration. She later returned to America where she worked for Morgan College and studied at the Howard School of Music. In 1932, she wrote the opera *Tom Tom: An Epic of Music and the Negro,* which focuses on four West African characters to illustrate the story of African American slavery and freedom. It is now referred to as the first race opera, and it received excellent reviews, with 10,000 people attending the premiere.

Apart from her compositions and theatre work, Du Bois wrote many books on influential Black people including Ghana's first prime minister, Kwame Nkrumah, and the scientist and inventor George Washington Carver.

You might recognise Shirley's last name. That's because she was married to the author, sociologist and activist W.E.B. Du Bois!

AVRIL COLERIDGE-TAYLOR
(1903–98)
South Norwood, London, UK

It seems Coleridge-Taylor followed in the footsteps of her father, the famous composer Samuel Coleridge-Taylor! At 12, she wrote her first piece, called 'Goodbye Butterfly'. Later, after winning a scholarship to study piano and composition, she went on to study at London's Trinity College of Music.

She became the first woman to conduct the H.M.S Royal Marines and founded the Coleridge-Taylor Symphony Orchestra in the 1940s. During her career, she conducted both the London Symphony Orchestra and BBC Orchestra on numerous occasions. Because of apartheid in South Africa, once it was discovered that her grandfather was from Sierra Leone, Coleridge-Taylor was banned from conducting there. As a result of this, and facing discrimination as a Black woman in the UK, she occasionally composed under the name Peter Riley so that people would appreciate her music without any bias.

In 1957, she wrote the 'Ceremonial March' in commemoration of Ghana's independence from the British colonial rule. In total, she wrote more than 90 musical works, as well as a book about her father, *The Heritage of Samuel Coleridge-Taylor* (1979).

'Idylle for flute and piano, Op. 21' (1923)

Wyndore (1936)

Sussex Landscape, Op. 27 (1940)

UNDINE SMITH MOORE
(1904–89)
Jarratt, Virginia, U.S.A.

Moore grew up in a musical family and started taking piano lessons when she was 7. Later, she was the first student from the historically black Fisk University to be awarded a scholarship to the prestigious Juilliard School of Music, which allowed her to continue her studies there.

Moore became known as an important educator, travelling the US and lecturing about Black composers. She won many awards including the Virginia Governors Award, was named the Music Laureate of the state of Virginia, and received an honorary doctorate from Indiana University. Her composition *Scenes from the Life of a Martyr* was nominated for the Pulitzer Prize in 1981, and yet many of her compositions were only published after she died.

Q2: Whose life is 'Scenes from the Life of a Martyr' based on?
a) Dr. Martin Luther King Jr
b) Carol McNair
c) Emmett Till d) Malcolm X

'Valse Caprice' (1930)

'Before I'd be a Slave' (1953)

'Watch and Pray' (1972)

IRENE BRITTON SMITH
(1907–99)
Chicago, Illinois, U.S.A.

'Invention in Two Voices' (1940)

Dream Cycle (1947)

Sinfonietta (1956)

Smith was of mixed African and Native American descent, and she grew up hearing her mother play hymns on the piano, and soon she was composing her own tunes. She learned to play the violin and eventually became a part of the all-Black Harrison Ferrel Symphony Orchestra in 1930. She studied music theory and composed works such as *Passacaglia and Fugue in C# Minor* (1940) and *Sonata for Violin and Piano* (1947).

Smith was a lifelong learner and studied composition for many years, including spending a summer with Nadia Boulanger (who had also taught composers such as Aaron Copeland, Astor Piazzolla and Philip Glass) in France in 1958. She was an influential teacher and taught at many schools throughout the United States. Even though she stopped composing in 1962 and retired from teaching in 1978, her compositions have been performed and recorded by the likes of pianist Helen Walker-Hill and singer Theodore Stone.

ZENOBIA POWELL PERRY
(1908–2004)
Boley, Oklahoma, U.S.A.

While very young, Perry met the legendary educator and adviser to many U.S. presidents, Booker T. Washington. She had only been playing the piano for a few years when she won her first competition and decided to pursue a career in music. After completing her schooling, she moved to New York to study privately with another African American composer, Robert Nathaniel Dett.

Perry was active in the American civil rights movement, and she joined the NAACP (National Association for the Advancement of Colored People) in 1962. In 1985, she composed *Tawawa House*, which has become one of her most popular works. She won many awards, including a Music Citation for distinguished service in 1987, a Woman of the Year Award in 1999, and the Ohio Cultural Arts Award for outstanding contribution in 2002.

'De Angels Done Bowed Down' (1969)

'Flight' (1970)

'Sunset' (1977)

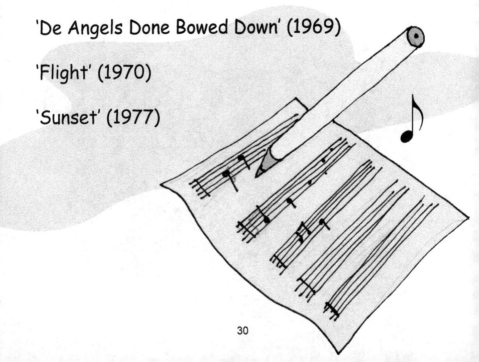

EVELYN LA RUE PITTMAN
(1910-92)
McAlester, Oklahoma U.S.A.

Pittman showed an interest in music from a very young age, and she started composing at about 6 years old. After studying for her master's degree at Oklahoma University, she moved to New York to study composition at Juilliard School of Music. Like Margaret Bonds, Julia Perry and others before her, she travelled to Paris to study with the famous composition teacher Nadia Boulanger. Some of Pittman's most well-known compositions are 'Rock-a-mah Soul' (1952) and her opera written about the life of Dr. Martin Luther King Jr, *Freedom Child* (1970).

MARY LOU WILLIAMS
(1910-81)
Atlanta, Georgia, U.S.A.

Williams started playing the piano when she was only 3, and she became known in her local area as 'The Little Piano Girl'. During her performing and recording career, she worked with many jazz musicians, including saxophonist Ben Webster, pianist Thelonious Monk, and drummer Art Blakey. After becoming Roman Catholic in 1956, she composed hymns and masses that focused on her new faith. Pieces such as 'Black Christ of the Andes', 'The Devil' (1963) and the album *Mary Lou's Mass* (1975) showed her ability to compose in different styles.

MARGARET BONDS
(1913–72)
Chicago, Illinois, U.S.A.

Bonds wrote her first piece, *Marquette Street Blues*, when she was only 5. Her mother was her first piano teacher, but she received composition lessons with Florence Price when she was still in school. As a singer, at the Chicago's World's Fair in 1933, she became the first Black soloist to perform with the Chicago Symphony. After receiving her master's degree, she had a successful career as a pianist and even performed Florence Price's *Piano Concerto* in 1934. During this time, her composing skills became so advanced that when she showed Nadia Boulanger her piece *The Negro Speaks of Rivers*, Ms. Boulanger told her that she didn't need to study with her!

In 1965, Bonds wrote *Montgomery Variations* (for orchestra) and dedicated it to Dr. Martin Luther King Jr. She was close friends with Langston Hughes, and they collaborated on a few pieces together. She won many awards including the Wanamaker Prize in 1932 and the Alumni Merit Award from Northwestern University in 1967.

The Ballad of the Brown King (1954)

Joshua Fit De Battle of Jericho (1959)

'Troubled Water' (1967)

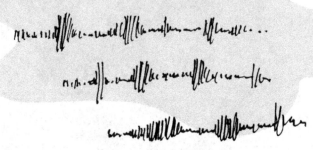

EMAHOY TSEGUÉ-MARYAM GUÈBROU
(born 1923)
Addis Ababa, Ethiopia

Guèbrou, an Ethiopian nun, was born into a wealthy family. She first discovered her love for music while studying at a boarding school in Switzerland. Upon joining the order of nuns, she gave up a budding career as a pianist but went on to compose many works. Most of the proceeds from their sales have gone to orphanages and charities in Ethiopia.

Did you know? Emperor Haile Selassie helped Guèbrou to record and release her first album in 1967.

JULIA PERRY
(1924–79)
Lexington, Kentucky, U.S.A.

Perry pursued her musical education while traveling throughout Europe, studying with world-renowned teacher and composer Nadia Boulanger in France, and Luigi Dallapiccola in Italy. One of her most famous pieces is called 'Stabat Mater', which was composed in 1951.

Perry taught at Florida A&M University starting in 1959, the same year she composed her Vivaldi-inspired *Requiem for Orchestra*. She later taught at Atlanta University. In total, she wrote 12 symphonies and 3 operas, as well as many other works that unfortunately have not been recorded. In 1971, she suffered a stroke that paralysed the right side of her body, but she learnt how to write with her left hand and carried on composing until her death in 1979.

'Prelude for Piano' (1946)

'Homunculus' (1960)

Piano Concerto (1964)

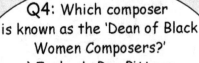

Q4: Which composer is known as the 'Dean of Black Women Composers?'
a) Evelyn LaRue Pittman
b) Avril Coleridge-Taylor
c) Julia Perry
d) Undine Smith Moore

MELBA LISTON (1926–99)

BETTY JACKSON KING (1928–94)

King earned her bachelor's and master's degrees in her hometown of Chicago, and she went on to compose many vocal pieces including 'In the Springtime' (1976). From 1970 to 1984, she served as the president of the National Association of Negro Musicians.

LENA MCLIN (born 1928)

During her many years of teaching in Chicago, McLin mentored many future famous musicians such as singers Chaka Khan, Robert Sims and rapper Da Brat. She has composed more than 400 works and co-founded the McLin Opera Company in order to help African Americans find a route into professional opera.

MICKI GRANT (born 1929)

DOLORES WHITE (born 1932)

VALERIE CAPERS (born 1935)

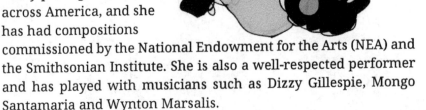

Capers was the first blind person to earn both a bachelor's and master's degree from the Juilliard School of Music in New York. She has taught at many prestigious schools across America, and she has had compositions commissioned by the National Endowment for the Arts (NEA) and the Smithsonian Institute. She is also a well-respected performer and has played with musicians such as Dizzy Gillespie, Mongo Santamaria and Wynton Marsalis.

JACQUELINE HAIRSTON (born 1938)

Hairston studied at Julliard and Howard University before becoming an award-winning ASCAP composer and arranger.

She has had works performed by the San Francisco Women's Orchestra and the London Symphony Orchestra, as well as winning the Howard Thurman award in 2014.

MARY WATKINS (born 1939)

Watkins, a graduate of historically Black Howard University, has had her compositions performed by many ensembles including The Women's Philharmonic Orchestra and The New Black Music Repertory Ensemble of Chicago. She has composed music for multiple films including *Freedom On My Mind*, which earned a Grammy nomination in 1994.

JEANNE LEE (1939–2000)

Lee grew up in a musical household in New York City and started her musical career as a performer. She toured Europe with the pianist Ran Blake in the 1960s, and upon returning to America, expanded her career to include composition. She composed 'In These Last Days' in 1973, and her oratorio 'Prayer for Our Time' was written in 1976 after she had worked with the composer John Cage. Lee continued to record and perform throughout her life, and she also wrote a jazz history textbook for children.

DOROTHY RUDD MOORE
(born 1940)
New Castle, Delaware, U.S.A.

Moore made up her own songs as a child, and her parents supported her dream of becoming a composer. She learned to play the clarinet and piano, and she graduated from Howard University in 1963. At 16, she wrote her first piece, 'Flight', which was inspired by the composer and pianist Duke Ellington. Like many before her, right after leaving Howard, Moore moved to Paris to study with legendary composition teacher Nadia Boulanger. Upon her return to the States, she lived in New York, where, in 1968, she and her husband would found the Society of Black Composers in order to help spread awareness of many talented Black composers.

Some of Moore's compositions focus specifically on the African American experience, including her opera *Frederick Douglass* (1985) partially based on the life of that historically important social reformer and slave abolitionist leader.

Songs from the Dark Tower (1970)

Transcension (1986)

Flowers of Darkness (1990)

JERALDINE SAUNDERS HERBISON (born 1941)

47

TANIA LEÓN
(born 1943)
Havana, Cuba

León started learning the piano at 4 in her native Havana. In 1967, she moved to New York, where two years later she helped to found the Arthur Mitchell's Dance Theatre of Harlem. She was commissioned to write the opera *Scourge of Hyacinths* in 1994, and she won the BMW Prize for Best New Opera.

León has won awards from the National Endowment for the Arts and the American Society of Composers, Authors and Publishers (ASCAP) as well as being awarded two honorary doctorates. In 1998, she was awarded the New York Governor's Lifetime Achievement Award, and she was named Distinguished Professor Emeritus by the City University of New York in 2006.

Batá (1985)

Horizons (1999)

Desde (2001)

JOYCE SOLOMON MOORMAN (born 1946)

ELEANOR ALBERGA
(born 1949)
Kingston, Jamaica

Alberga began composing when she was only 10, and at 21, she won a scholarship and moved to London to study at the Royal Academy of Music. While mainly performing as a concert pianist, she found herself composing more and more. In 1978, she became musical director of the London Contemporary Dance Theatre, and soon she was experimenting with rhythms influenced by her experience as a dancer. She composed her version of *Snow White and The Seven Dwarves* in 1994 and went on to win the NESTA Fellowship of composition award in 2001.

Alberga has had her music performed across the world, including her piece 'Arise Athena!', which opened the Last Night of the Proms in 2015 and was played by the BBC Symphony Orchestra. In 2020, she was awarded 'Fellow of the Royal Academy of Music'.

"I think I'm influenced by everything" - *Eleanor Alberga*

Q6: Who was the first Black woman to win a Grammy for the Best Musical Score Album?
a) Dorothy Rudd Moore
b) Micki Grant
c) Evelyn La Rue Pittman
d) Undine Smith Moore

String Quartet No.1 (1993)

The Wild Blue Yonder (1995)

'If The Silver Bird Could Speak' (1996)

CYNTHIA COZETTE LEE
(born 1953)
Pittsburgh, Pennsylvania, U.S.A.

Cozette learnt several instruments in her childhood, and at 15, she composed a piece called *The Nymph* for a Pittsburgh Flute Club Composition competition. She concentrated on playing the flute and studied composition at Jacksonville University, and later at the Juilliard School of Music.

In the early 1980s, she produced her own classical music radio show where she interviewed African American classical musicians in Philadelphia. She won a College Music Society Composition Award for *Nigerian Treasures for Solo Unaccompanied Flute* in 1985, which had its first performance in Canada. She has composed a range of works, including four operas, pieces for chamber orchestra, musicals, and choral works.

The Black Guitar (1982)

Songs I Wrote For Broadway (2001)

Ebony Reflections for Chamber Orchestra

"If Marian Anderson
or Paul Robeson or composers
Julia Perry or William Grant
Still had given up then
there would be
no Cynthia Cozette Lee"

- *Cynthia Cozette Lee*

EVELYN SIMPSON-CURENTON (born 1953)

LESA TERRY (born 1955)

Q7: Who conducted the Broadway production of The Wiz in 1992?
a) Tania León b) Errollyn Wallen
c) Pamela Z
d) Dorothy Rudd Moore

REGINA HARRIS BAIOCCHI
(born 1956)
Chicago, Illinois, U.S.A.

Baiocchi began to compose at an early age, and her interest in music inspired her to learn several instruments including the French horn, recorder and guitar. She graduated from Chicago's Roosevelt University with a bachelor's degree in music. Her first opera, *Gbeldahoven: No One's Child*, was composed in 1996, and in 1997, she composed, conducted and directed the music for a play titled *Nikki Giovanni*.

In addition to composing instrumental and choral music, Baiocchi founded the Haiku Festival to help promote children reading and writing. She has won many accolades including the Chicago Music Association award in 1995, has performed around the world and has several articles published in *Black Women in America: An Historical Encyclopaedia*.

QFX (1993)

African Hands (1997)

'Azuretta' (2000)

PAMELA Z
(born 1956)
Buffalo, New York, U.S.A.

Pamela Z is a composer who works with her voice, often in live settings, using loops, samples and other electronic techniques. She became active on the contemporary music scene in the 1980s and has been performing regularly around the world ever since. She has composed music for Eighth Blackbird, the Kronos Quartet and Stephan Koplowitz, as well as creating sonic installations at places such as the Trondheim Elektroniske Kunstsenter in Norway, and the Dakar Biennale in Senegal. Among her many achievements are the Herb Alpert Award, the Guggenheim Fellowship and the Rome Prize.

Pop Titles 'You' (1986)

'Obsession, Addiction and the Aristotelian Curve' (1993)

Ethel Dreams of Temporal Disturbances (2005)

SHIRLEY J. THOMPSON
(born 1958)
London, U.K.

Thompson is an award-winning British composer of Jamaican descent. In 2002, she became the first woman in forty years to have composed and conducted her own symphony. Titled *New Nation Rising, A 21st Century Symphony*, it was commissioned for Queen Elizabeth II's Golden Jubilee. Her solo cello and string orchestral dance score *Shift* is part of the award-winning ballet called *PUSH*, which has been performed all over the world.

Thompson has been named one of Britain's top 100 most-influential people of African or African Caribbean descent every year since 2010 (Powerlist). She was the first female executive of the Association of Professional Composers and currently lectures at the University of Westminster in London.

'The Woman Who Refused to Dance' was inspired by the true story of a Black woman who was beaten and murdered for refusing to dance while on a boat from Calabar (modern day Nigeria) to Grenada in 1792.

A Child of the Jago (1997)

Spirit Songs (2007)

The Woman Who Refused to Dance (2007)

ERROLLYN WALLEN
(born 1958)
Belize

Wallen was born in Belize but moved to London at a young age. In 1998, she became the first Black woman to have her work performed at the BBC Proms. She studied at Kings College in London before going on to earn a master's in Philosophy at Cambridge University. In 2006, Wallen co-wrote a song with an astronaut on a Space Shuttle on the way to the International Space Station! She was awarded an MBE (Member of the Order of the British Empire) for her contribution to music in 2007 and was commissioned to compose for the 2012 Paralympics opening ceremony. In 2017, Wallen wrote *Mighty River*, which commemorated the 1807 abolition of England's slave trade. She was awarded a CBE in 2020 and has recorded with musicians such as Sting and Björk in her career to date. Also in 2020, her arrangement of the song 'Jerusalem', featured in the last night of the BBC Proms.

Dervish (2001)

Spirit In Motion (2012)

Cello Concerto (2016)

ROSENPHAYNE POWELL (born 1962)

Powell is well known as a prolific composer of vocal music. A lot of her music has been published and performed around the world, and in 2009, at the California State University African Diaspora Sacred Music Festival, she received the Living Legend Award.

VALERIE COLEMAN (born 1970)

By the time she was 14, Coleman had already written three symphonies and was playing the flute in a youth orchestra. She earned her master's degree in flute performance and became the first Black woman to be commissioned to compose for the Philadelphia Orchestra. The *Washington Post* newspaper named Coleman as one of the Top 35 female composers in classical music.

JERI LYNNE JOHNSON (born 1972)

VALERIE
COLEMAN

NKEIRU OKOYE
(born 1972)
New York, New York, U.S.A.

Okoye grew up in the United States but spent time in Nigeria as a child. She began composing in her early teens and later graduated from the Oberlin Conservatory of Music in 1993. Some of her most famous works include *Voices Shouting Out* (2002) and the opera *Harriet Tubman: When I Crossed That Line to Freedom* (2014). In 2018, Okoye wrote an orchestral piece called *Charlotte Mecklenberg*, a direct reference to Keith Lamont Scott, who was fatally shot by a police officer (in Charlotte) on 20 September 2016.

Okoye has won many awards including an ASCAP Grant for Young Composers for her piece *The Genesis* (1995). She sits on the board of Composers Now and has been commissioned by organisations such as the John Duffy Composer Institute and the Walt Whitman Project.

Q8:
The earliest known piano solo to be composed by a Black woman was by written by who in 1893?
a) Catalina Berroa b) Amanda Aldridge
c) Estelle Ricketts
d) Anna Goodwin

TEBOGO MONNAKGOTLA (born 1972)

Monnakgotla has been called 'one of the most prominent Swedish composers of her generation'. She studied composition at the Royal College of Music in Stockholm, and she won the Carin Malmlöf-Forssling Prize in 2017. In 2018, she was nominated for a Nordic Council Music Prize for her opera *Jean-Joseph*.

TOMEKA REID (born 1977)
CHANDA DANCY (born 1978)
LORI HICKS (born 1979)

EDEWEDE ORIWOH (born 1981)

Oriwoh is a Nigerian composer who has written vocal music in six languages including Yoruba, German and Latin. In 2017, she won the Panache Global Entertainment Award for outstanding achievement in music and community development.

JESSIE MONTGOMERY (born 1981)

Montgomery's parents were heavily involved in the arts, and she learned to play the violin at an early age. She earned a master's degree in composition for film and multimedia in 2012. Her long involvement with The Sphinx Organisation has helped her both to record her first album, *Strum: Music for Strings* (2015), and to become a composer-in-residence for the Sphinx Virtuosi. Some of Montgomery's compositions have been performed by major ensembles including the Atlanta Symphony and Dallas Symphony orchestras, and she has been featured on national radio in the States. In 2017, she won the ASCAP Foundation Leonard Bernstein Composer Award, and she continues to perform, compose and teach aspiring violinists and composers.

HANNAH KENDALL (born 1984)

Kendall grew up in North London and studied composition at the University of Exeter before attending the Royal College of Music. In 2015, she was called one of the 'brilliant female composers under the age of 35', and that same year she won a Woman of the Future Award.

JESSICA MAYS (born 1987)
SHELLEY WASHINGTON (born 1991)

Did you know? Oriwoh isn't just a composer – she also has a PhD in Digital Forensics!

CASSIE KINOSHI
(born 1993)
Welwyn Garden City, Hertfordshire, UK

Soon after graduating from Trinity Laban Conservatoire, British composer Kinoshi began touring and recording with the bands Nérija and KOKOROKO. She was nominated for BBC Young Composer of the Year in 2012, and she formed an ensemble called SEED, which was nominated for a Mercury Award in 2019 for their album *Driftglass*. Kinoshi took part in the London Symphony Orchestra Panufnik Scheme in 2018–19, and she has composed extensively for theatre productions in the UK including for *Blue Beneath My Skin* (Bunker Theatre) and *SuperBlackMan* (Battersea Arts Centre).

'Run Sonic Run' (2014)

'The Dreamkeeper' (2015)

'Interplanetary Migration' (2017)

"I look forward to the day where skill set and hard work is solely valued before the gender, race or background of the composer in question."

Cassie Kinoshi

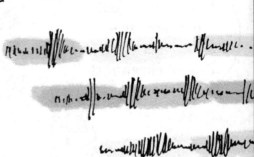

LAWREN BRIANNA WARE (1994)
JOCELYN CHAMBERS (1996)
ALLISON LOGGINS-HULL
AMANDA JONES
B.E. BOYKIN
CARMEN BROUARD
CHRISTEN HOLMES
CORIE ROSE SOUMAH
COURTNEY BRYAN
DAIJANA WALLACE
DIEDRE MURRAY
EDEWEDE ORIWOH
ELIZABETH A. BAKER
ELLA JARMAN PINTO
JANAÉ E.
JASMINE BARNES
JESSICA MAYS
LEILA ADU
LINDA K TWINE
MARIA CORLEY
MAYEN MEIMEI AKPAN
MAZZ SWIFT
NAILAH NOMBEKO
NOKUTHULA NGWENYAMA
PAMELA DILLARD
RENEE BAKER
TAMAR-KALI
SAKARI DIXON VANDERVEER
SHARON J. WILLIS
STEPHANIE FISCHER
YVETTE JANINE JACKSON
ZANAIDA ROBLES

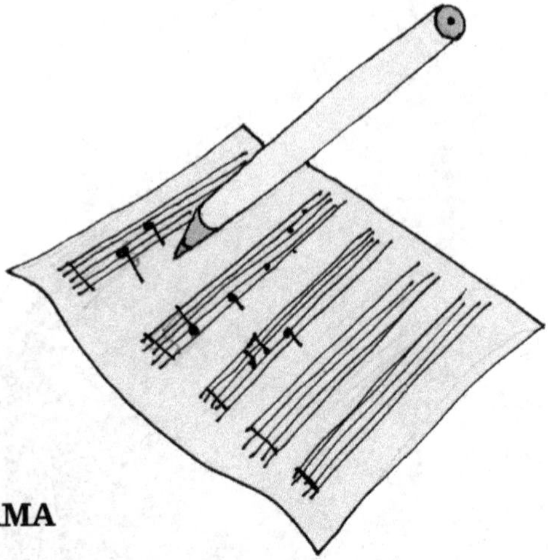

KATHRYN BOSTIC

Bostic is well known for her composition work on movies such as *Middle of Nowhere* (2012), *Dear White People* (2014), and *Toni Morrison: The Pieces I Am* (2019). In 2016, she became the first African American female score composer to join the Academy of Motion Picture Arts and Sciences.

ANSWERS

Q1 b) Marian Anderson
Q2 a) Dr. Martin Luther King Jr
Q3 c) Duke University
Q4 d) Undine Smith Moore
Q5 d) Clarinet
Q6 b) Micki Grant
Q7 a) Tania León
Q8 c) Estelle Ricketts

PLAYLIST

Concerto in C Minor - Helen Eugenia Hagan (1912)
Tom Tom: *An Epic of Music and the Negro* - Shirley Graham Du Bois (1932)
Short Piece for Orchestra - Julia Perry (1952)
Dances in the Canebrakes - Florence Price (1953)
3 Dream Portraits - Margaret Bonds (1959)
Éthiopiques 21: Piano Solo - Emahoy Tsegué-Maryam Guèbrou (1963)
Sing About Love - Valerie Capers (1974)
Blues Dialogues: II. Expressive - Dolores White (1988)
Sun Warrior - Eleanor Alberga (1990)
Wait Till I Put On My Crown - Lena McLin (1990)
'Bone Music' - Pamela Z (1992)
Para viola y Orquesta - Tania León (1995)
Umoja: The First Day of Kwanza - Valerie Coleman (1997)
Dusk - Nkeiru Okoye (2006)
'This Little Rose' - Ella Jarman-Pinto (2010)
Daedalus - Errollyn Wallen (2012)
The Cry of Jeremiah - Rosephanye Powell (2012)
'Asphalt Grandpa' - Leila Adu (2016)
Cape Coast Castle - Joyce Solomon Moorman (2016)
Jean-Joseph - Tebogo Monnakgotla (2016)
The Knife of Dawn - Hannah Kendall (2016)
Babe Ese - Edewede Oriwoh (2017)
Coincident Dances - Jessie Montgomery (2017)

Black Women Composers: A Century Of Piano Music (1893–1990) (1992)
Zodiac Suite - Mary Lou Williams (1945)

BOOKS

Black Women Composers: A Genesis - Mildred Denby Green (1983)

Jam!: The Story of Jazz Music - Jeanne Lee (1999)

Chiquinha Gonzaga - Coleção Crianças Famosas - Bonio Angelo (2001)
Race Woman: The Lives of Shirley Graham Du Bois - Gerald Horne (2002)

From Spirituals to Symphonies: African-American Women Composers and Their Music - Helen Walker-Hill (2007)

Music by Black Women Composers: A Bibliography of Available Scores - Helen Walker-Hill (2007)

American Composer Zenobia Powell Perry: Race and Gender in the 20th Century - Jeannie Gayle Pool (2008)

The Heart of a Woman - The Life and Music of Florence B. Price - Rae Linda Brown (2020)

ABOUT THE AUTHOR

Nathan Holder is a musician, author and consultant based in London. He received his master's degree in music performance from Kingston University, while winning the MMus Prize for Outstanding Achievement. As a musician, he has performed with artists such as Ed Sheeran, The Arkells and Zoe Birkett, and performed in locations in Dubai, Bali, the USA and across Europe. His first book, published in 2018, is titled I Wish I Didn't Quit: Music Lessons.

ABOUT THE ILLUSTRATOR

Charity Russell is a children's book author and illustrator. She was born in Zambia and after a bit of globe trotting growing up she moved to the U.K. where she made her home.

She studied illustration BA (hons) at Falmouth University College and later received a First Class Masters degree in Illustration and Design at The University of Sunderland.

She lives in Bristol, England with her husband, two children and Frank (the dog).

You can contact her at www.charityrussell.com

OTHER BOOKS
written by Nathan Holder

WWW.THEWHYBOOKS.CO.UK